BLAZERS

POO AND PUKE EATERS
OF THE ANIMAL WORLD

by Jody Sullivan Rake

Content Consultant:
David Stephens, PhD
Professor of Ecology, Evolution and Behaviour

Reading Consultant:
Professor Barbara J. Fox

raintree

a Capstone company — publishers for children

Raintree is an imprint of Capstone Global Library Limited, a company incorporated in England and Wales having its registered office at 7 Pilgrim Street, London, EC4V 6LB – Registered company number: 6695582

www.raintree.co.uk
myorders@raintree.co.uk

ISBN 978-1-4062-9176-6
18 17 16 15 14
10 9 8 7 6 5 4 3 2 1

British Library Cataloguing in Publication Data
A full catalogue record for this book is available from the British Library.

Editorial Credits
Abby Colich, editor; Kyle Grenz, designer; Jo Miller, media researcher; Katy LaVigne, production specialist

Photo Credits
Alamy: Arco Images GmbH/Delpho, M., 14-15, Ger Bosma, 8-9; Dreamstime: Henrikhl, 19 (inset); Getty Images: E+/Ivan Mayes, 22-23; Newscom: imago stock & people, 10-11; NOAA Okeanos Explorer Program, Galapagos Rift Expedition 2011, 20-21; Science Source: Scimat, 28-29; Shutterstock: Aaron Welch, 4-5, Emily Veinglory, 8 (inset), Johan Swanepoel, cover, john michael evan potter, 16-17, K&D Foster Photographers, 12-13, NagyDodo, 18-19, NattapolStudiO, 7 (inset), Patrick Poendl, 24-25, withGod, 26-27; SuperStock: Biosphoto, 6-7

Printed in China by Nordica.
1014/CA21401515

CONTENTS

THEY EAT WHAT?

All animals must eat to survive. Some animal **diets** are unusual. Others are just disgusting! What are the most disgusting things animals eat? They just might be poo and puke!

rhinoceros

diet what an animal eats

Fact!

Poo is also known as waste, droppings, faeces and dung. Puke is also called sick and vomit.

Why poo and puke? Poo and puke contain partly **digested** bits of food. These bits have **nutrients** that many animals need. Animals may also be protecting themselves or their young by eating poo and puke.

digest break down food so it can be used by the body

nutrient part of food, such as a vitamin, that is used for growth and health

guinea
fowl

elephant
dung

rabbit
pellets

RABBIT HABIT

Rabbits are plant eaters. These animals poo out **pellets** of half-digested plants. They nibble the pellets to get much-needed nutrients. Later, the rabbits make new poo without nutrients. They don't eat this new poo.

SALTY SNACKS

Gorillas and chimpanzees eat their own poo for the same reason as rabbits. They find seeds and other undigested bits of food in their poo. Poo also contains salt. Salt helps gorillas and chimpanzees to keep their bodies healthy.

Fact!

Scientists study animal poo. The poo helps them to learn about the animals' diet and health.

MOTHER'S MANURE

Elephant and hippo babies eat their mothers' poo. These babies are born without the **bacteria** they need to digest food. The poo has the bacteria elephant and hippo babies need.

Fact!

An elephant may poo up to 36 kilograms (80 pounds) of waste each day!

bacteria very small living things that exist everywhere

KEEPING IT CLEAN

Wolf and cougar mothers may eat their babies' poo. Eating the babies' poo helps to keep their dens clean. Mothers also eat poo to stop **predators** from picking up the **scent**.

predator animal that hunts other animals for food
scent smell of something

Fact!
Pet cats are related to wild cats. Sometimes mother cats eat their kittens' poo.

DUNG AT HEART

Dung beetles are named after their disgusting diet. Dung beetles fly around looking for fresh poo. But they are fussy poo-eaters. They prefer the poo of **herbivores**.

Fact!

Dung beetles help new trees to grow. When they bury their dung balls, seeds in the dung can sprout and grow.

herbivore animal that eats only plants

There are three different types of dung beetle. Rollers form dung into a ball and use it as food. They also mate and lay eggs in the dung. Tunnellers dig into dung where they make a new home. Dwellers live right on top of piles of poo.

dung beetle young

Fact!
In one night, a roller dung beetle can bury 250 times its own weight in poo.

PLENTY OF POO IN THE SEA

The sea is full of murky clouds of **detritus**. Detritus includes bits of food left by other animals. It also contains the poo of sea creatures. Many sea animals depend on detritus for their food.

Fact!

As detritus sinks deeper into the sea, it becomes known as "marine snow". Marine snow is food for many animals in the sun-less deep sea.

detritus bits of food and animal poo that floats through the sea

21

DOGGIE DOO-DOO

Have you ever seen a pet dog eat its own poo? Dogs may eat poo because their wolf relatives do. Or they may be lacking nutrients in their diet.

Fact!

Dogs often eat too quickly. When this happens, the stomach sometimes sends food back up. The sick may become another meal for the dog.

BABY FOOD FOR BIRDS

Most baby birds stay in the nest while their parents find food. Not all bird parents can carry food back in their feet or beaks. So they swallow the food and then vomit it into the chicks' mouths.

CHEW ON THIS

Cows chew on a ball of sick called **cud**. Sheep, goats and camels chew cud, too. These animals chew grass until it is wet with spit. The food is swallowed and softened in the stomach. Then it comes back up to the mouth for more chewing.

Fact!

Cows and other cud-chewers have four stomachs. Each stomach has a special job in the digestion of grass.

cud food that has not been digested

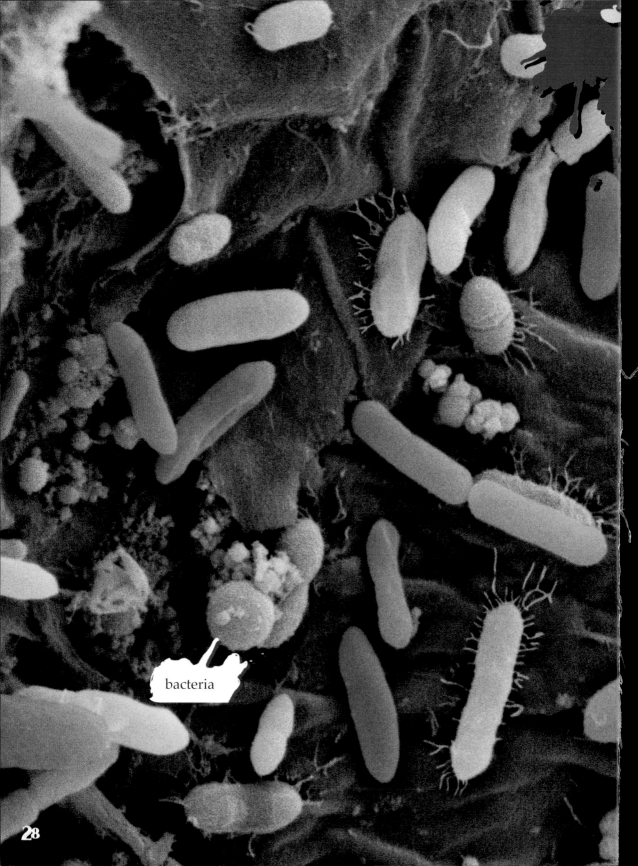

bacteria

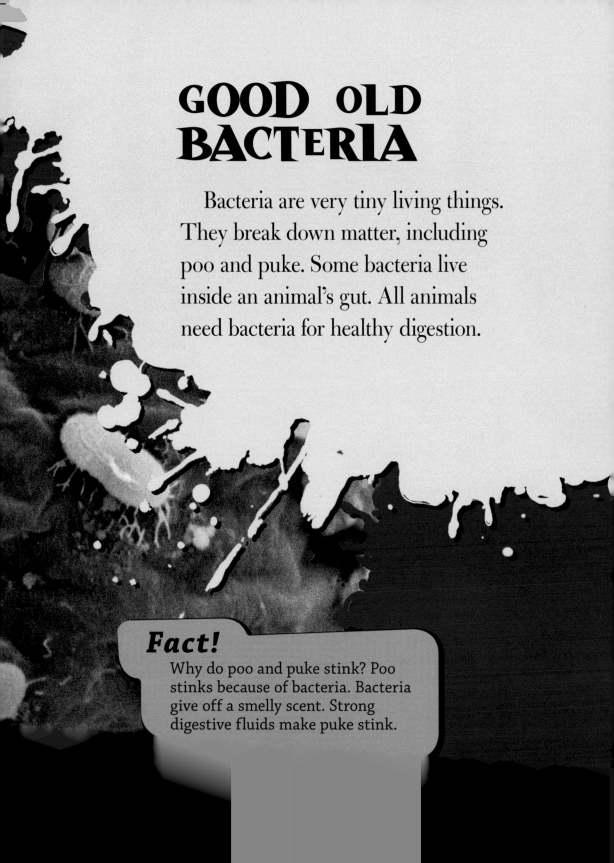

GOOD OLD BACTERIA

Bacteria are very tiny living things. They break down matter, including poo and puke. Some bacteria live inside an animal's gut. All animals need bacteria for healthy digestion.

Fact!

Why do poo and puke stink? Poo stinks because of bacteria. Bacteria give off a smelly scent. Strong digestive fluids make puke stink.

GLOSSARY

bacteria   very small living things that exist everywhere

cud   food that has not been digested

detritus   bits of food and animal poo that floats through the sea

diet   what an animal eats

digest   break down food so it can be used by the body

herbivore   animal that eats only plants

malnutrition   condition caused by a lack of healthy food in the diet

nutrient   part of food, such as a vitamin, that is used for growth and health

pellet   small, round piece of poo

predator   animal that hunts other animals for food

scent   smell of something

READ MORE

Dogs (Animal Abilities), Charlotte Guillain (Raintree, 2014)

Gorillas (Living in the Wild: Primates), Lori McManus (Raintree, 2012)

Life Processes (Essential Life Science), Richard and Louise Spilsbury (Raintree, 2014)

That's Life, Robert Winston (Dorling Kindersley, 2012)

WEBSITES

www.bbc.co.uk/nature/life/Dung_beetle
Watch videos and find out more fascinating facts about this tiny but mighty dung eater.

www.bbc.co.uk/nature/life/Elephantidae
Is the water found in elephant dung really good enough to drink? Find out this answer and more.

INDEX